Celebrating your year

1953

a very special year for

A message from the author:

Welcome to the year 1953.

I trust you will enjoy this fascinating romp down memory lane.

And when you have reached the end of the book, please join me in the battle against AI generated copy-cat books and fake reviews.

Details are at the back of the book.*

Best regards,
Bernard Bradforsand-Tyler.

Contents

1953 American Family Life	9
Austerity in the United Kingdom	13
The Queen is Crowned	17
Our Love Affair with Cars	19
The Golden Age of Television	23
Most Popular TV Shows of 1953	24
Eisenhower Inaugurated	28
Death of a Dictator	29
East German Uprising	31
Armistice Ends War in Korea	32
Threat of Nuclear War	36
Execution of the Rosenbergs	37
1953 in Cinema and Film	40
Top Grossing Films of the Year	41
1953 Sci-Fi Inspired Films	43
James Bond 007 in Print	45
Musical Memories	46
1953 Billboard Top 30 Songs	48
Fashion Trends of the 1950s	52
A Vaccine for Polio	62
Technology and Medicine	63
Sporting Events from 1953	66
Everest Conquered	67
Other News from 1953	68
Famous People Born in 1953	72
1953 in Numbers	76
Image Attributions	84

Advertisement

" '*Hey, Mother!*' Susan called out, 'guess what country has the heaviest rainfall in the world!' "For all *I* knew it was Timbuktu... so I said, 'I give up, Sue. What's the answer?' Sue looked pleased and held up a World Book volume, 'It's a province in India called Assam, World Book says. It's about the size of Iowa.'

Then she went on to tell how rain is formed and why some parts of the earth have a great deal while other parts have very little.

"I watched her eager face and remembered how a year ago we'd called her 'Lazy Susan.' But thanks to World Book, there she was, full of interest—and she didn't even think of it as 'studying'! Once again, World Book had succeeded in helping Sue really to enjoy learning."

Parents in 9 out of 10 "World Book homes" report their children do better school work. And World Book becomes a real part of family life—gives Dad information on aviation or sports or politics, settles dinner-table discussions and starts new ones going! Bring World Book Encyclopedia into *your* home—and soon!

19 VOLUMES DELUXE EDITION $129.00
$10 down $6 a month

More families buy **World Book** than any other **ENCYCLOPEDIA**

1st Choice of America's Schools and Libraries! *Ask any teacher or librarian.*

SEND NOW FOR FREE BOOKLET!
Write today for your copy of valuable free booklet, "How to Help Your Child Win Success." Address: Mr. George M. Hayes, World Book, Dept. 115, Box 3565, Chicago 54, Illinois.

Name_____

" '*Hey, Mother!*' Susan called out, 'guess what country has the heaviest rainfall in the world!' "For all *I* knew it was Timbuktu... so I said, 'I give up, Sue. What's the answer?' Sue looked pleased and held up a World Book volume, 'It's a province in India called Assam, World Book says. It's about the size of Iowa.'

Then she went on to tell how rain is formed and why some parts of the earth have a great deal while other parts have very little.

"I watched her eager face and remembered how a year ago we'd called her 'Lazy Susan.' But thanks to World Book, there she was, full of interest–and she didn't even think of it as 'studying'! Once again, World Book had succeeded in helping Sue really to enjoy learning."

Parents in 9 out of 10 "World Book homes" report their children do better school work. And World Book becomes a real part of family life–gives Dad information on aviation or sports or politics, settles dinner-table discussions and starts new ones going! Bring World Book Encyclopedia into *your* home–and soon!

19 Volumes Deluxe Edition $129.00 $10 down $6 a month

More families buy World Book than any other encyclopedia

1st Choice of America's Schools and Libraries! *Ask any teacher or librarian.*

Let's flashback to 1953, a very special year.

Was this the year you were born?

Was this the year you were married?

Whatever the reason, this book is a celebration of your year,

THE YEAR 1953.

Turn the pages to discover a book packed with fun-filled fabulous facts. We look at the people, the places, the politics and the pleasures that made 1953 unique and helped shape the world we know today.

So get your time-travel suit on, and enjoy this trip down memory lane, to rediscover what life was like, back in the year 1953.

Advertisement

Secretary

To busy executive. Interesting work. Pleasant surroundings, modern office, including IBM Electric Typewriter. Write Box M2345

"that's the job for me!"

Other things being equal, what girl wouldn't prefer a job that includes an IBM Electric Typewriter? It's so easy to use and turns out such beautiful letters and reports.

With an IBM, you'll do your typing almost effortlessly, and with no errors due to fatigue.

To the executive, an IBM means faster typing, and better-looking letters that are a pleasure to sign.

For illustrated brochure, write or telephone your nearest IBM office.

1953 American Family Life

Imagine if time-travel was a reality, and one fine morning you wake up to find yourself flashed back in time, back to the year 1953.

What would life be like for a typical family, in a typical town, somewhere in America?

The post-war boom continued throughout the entire decade of the '50s. And with the booming economy, came booming birth numbers, booming suburbs, and the booming trappings of the consumerist culture we still live in today.

Our rising middle classes were feeling cashed-up. With an increasing desire to spend and to own, consumer demand continued to reach new highs year after year.

An unprecedented 3.97 million babies were born in 1953 (up from 2.8 million at the end of the war seven years earlier).[1]

To cater to the increase in demand, new houses were built in record numbers, most of them in the new suburban developments springing up on the outskirts of towns. Home sales were boosted by returned soldiers who had access to low interest loans through the G.I. Bill (1944-1956). A house in the suburbs had become the American dream for white middle-class families.

The family was everything. Fathers commuted to earn a salary. Wives were encouraged to quit their jobs and stay at home. Children walked to school and played outdoors in their well manicured gardens.

Relaxing in the sun—
American suburbs in the '50s.

Families dined together, watched television together, and enjoyed leisure time and outings together.

The average family income was $4,200 a year.[2] Unemployment rose to 4.5%, with GDP growth at 4.7%.[3]

Average costs in 1953 [4]	
New house	$18,159
Television	$200
Refrigerator	$450
A gallon of gasoline	$0.29

[1] U.S. Census Bureau *Estimates of the Population of the United States*: 1950-1954, page 2.
[2] census.gov/library/publications/1954/demo/p60-015.html.
[3] thebalance.com/unemployment-rate-by-year-3305506.
[4] thepeoplehistory.com and mclib.info/reference/local-history-genealogy/historic-prices/.

Joining the TV in our families' list of must-haves were: fully-automatic washing machines, defrost refrigerators, front-loading dryers, vacuum cleaners, air-conditioning and heating units, milkshake makers, and a multitude of other fancy kitchen gadgets and home appliances. In addition, every respectable family needed a car or two, motorcycles, bicycles, hiking/ camping/ picnic gear, and much, much more. An energetic and persuasive advertising industry, through TV, radio and print, ensured we always knew what our next purchase should be.

General Electric *Stratoliner Home Electric Unit* magazine advertisement from 1953.

A safety education magazine cover from the '50s.

But beneath the appearance of abundance and domestic bliss, Americans were deeply concerned. The Soviets had detonated an atomic bomb in 1949, setting in motion a Nuclear Arms Race between the two superpowers—the Cold War.

The USA created an even more powerful device—the hydrogen bomb, and the Soviets would soon build their own.

We would endure nearly four more decades of tension between the two super-powers before the Cold War finally ended in 1991 with the dissolution of the Soviet Union.

Advertisement

Here's the only laundry unit ever developed to dry as well as wash your clothes automatically... in one continuous operation. A single setting of the Duomatic dials and your clothes are thoroughly washed, then completely dried... while you're away... while you play... while you sleep. No watching, no waiting, no worrying. You're finished with your washday in seconds.

The Duomatic washes your clothes in warm or hot water... spins water out of clothes evenly, safely... triple rinses with clean, fresh water... and completely drys them—all automatically. In addition, you have an automatic speed-soak that takes only a few minutes for even the grimiest clothes.

Before you even consider buying any washer or dryer, you owe it to yourself to see the Bendix Duomatic. See a Free Demonstration.

Install Anywhere—no vent necessary for drying. No bolting down needed because "Balanced Action" eliminates vibration. And the Duomatic takes just half the space of separate washers and dryers.

Cleaner Clothes—exclusive Magic Heater makes wash water hotter, keeps it hot, gets clothes cleaner.

Economical—uses less water and soap than most ordinary automatic washers.

Austerity in the United Kingdom

Now just imagine you flashed back to a town in 1953 United Kingdom or Western Europe.

Unlike boom-time America, a very different, more restrained lifestyle would await you.

1953 was a year to mark new beginnings and new hopes for the future. The British crowned a new queen, and the 14-year-long rationing of sugar and sweets was finally lifted.

After the devastating deadly smog of the previous year, that claimed more than 10,000 lives, and the death of their beloved monarch—King George VI, the British populace needed some collective cheering up. The Coronation of Queen Elizabeth II brought pride, joy and unity to the citizens. It was an extravagance of pomp and ceremony, and the first ever to be televised.

The Gold State Coach on Coronation Day, 2nd June 1953.

London, like many other major European cities, bore the brunt of destruction from WWII bombings. Reconstruction was painfully slow, hampered by a general shortage of money, manpower and materials.

In cities there was a desperate shortage of housing to accommodate the growing population. Nearly half of those in cities lived in private, rented, often substandard apartments. While in the country, homes often lacked water, sanitation, electricity and phones.

Aerial view of London showing bombed areas in the foreground, 1953.

Stifling and miserable austerity measures, in place since the start of the war, were slowly being lifted. By 1953, most items were available for purchase without coupons, however rationing of meat would continue for another year.

British children at school in the early '50s.

The post-war baby boom, along with the shortage of funds and building materials for new schools, often resulted in crowded classes of up to 50 students in urban areas.

Winston Churchill, UK Prime Minister from 1940-1945, returned for a second term in 1951 at almost 77 years old.

By 1953, his health had deteriorated, however plans to step aside in favour of his Foreign Secretary, Anthony Eden, were derailed when Eden fell seriously ill. Churchill increased his workload, taking on foreign office duties to cover for Eden.

On 23rd June, Churchill suffered a stroke causing partial paralysis. With Eden incapacitated, Churchill's stroke was kept hidden from the public.

Churchill with Queen Elizabeth II, Prince Charles and Princess Anne, 10th Feb 1953.

For services to the country during the war years, Churchill was granted the *Most Noble Order of the Garter,* and knighted as Sir Winston on 24th Apr 1953. In recognition of his written works, including historical accounts of the wars and his arresting speeches, Churchill received a Nobel Prize in Literature on 10th Dec 1953.

Churchill worked tirelessly to develop a "special relationship" between the USA and the UK, based on their common distrust of communism, and recognizing America's financial assistance to a post-war bankrupt Britain. The substantial loans were finally paid back in full in 2006.

Lack of excess cash reserves made it increasingly difficult for the UK to continue financing and keeping secure its far-flung colonies. As a result, many British colonies would be released during the following 10 years, gaining independence as new nations. The United Kingdom was quickly losing its super-power status on the world's stage.

Advertisement

Get Ready for vacation pleasure!... with relaxed, scenic Greyhound trips to anywhere in America.

Now's the time to plan if you want to pack every minute of vacation time with relaxation, fun, and adventure! The place to get complete, helpful information is your nearest Greyhound ticket office. Greyhound Travel Bureaus, in all principal cities, will help arrange every detail of your trip—even make hotel reservations.

Get Set for travel savings!... with pre-planned Expense-Paid Vacation Tours...
These delightful tours—and hundreds more—include hotels, sightseeing, transportation.

Go Greyhound!... the one sure way to have a glorious vacation!
You're off to a winning start when you step aboard a Greyhound coach, enroute to Vacationland, U.S.A.! Getting there and back is a scenic treat (optional routes going and coming)—and you're totally free from driving strain. Dollars saved by Greyhound give you extra days of pleasure. Scores of Greyhound schedules take you *straight through* by most direct routes, without change of bus or baggage.

Big News! The world's most amazing motor coach, Greyhound's new Highway Traveler eliminates conventional steel springs, floats bus passengers on cushions of air. Hundreds of these new coaches, with advanced air conditioning, now in operation.

The Queen is Crowned

2nd June 1953

The coronation of Queen Elizabeth II was held on 2nd June 1953, 16 months after the sudden and unexpected passing of her father King George VI. The delay allowed time for preparations, with her husband Philip, Duke of Edinburgh, leading the Coronation Committee.

The Queen rode the 18th century Gold State Coach to Westminster Abbey for the Coronation. After the event, a 5 miles (8.0 km) procession brought her coach along London's crowd-filled landmark streets back to Buckingham Palace.

750 commentators broadcast in 39 languages along the procession route. It was the first major event to be televised worldwide. BBC footage was flown direct to the USA and Canada for same day broadcast. Footage was also dispatched to Australia, reaching Sydney in a record time of 53 hours 28 minutes.

Coronation portrait of Queen Elizabeth II wearing her Coronation Robe and Crown, and carrying the Orb and Scepter, 2nd June 1953.

The procession included British Empire and Commonwealth military personnel, British and foreign royalty, and heads of state.

Within Westminster Abbey, 8,000 guests witnessed the Coronation–part religious, part regal–in keeping with the centuries old traditions.

Queen Elizabeth II ruled until her death on 8th Sept 2022, making her the longest serving monarch in British history.

Coronation portrait of Queen Elizabeth II with Philip, Duke of Edinburgh, 2nd June '53.

Advertisement

We seldom see a motorist so surprised or so delighted as when he takes his first ride behind the wheel of a new Cadillac. For, in that single journey, he discovers power and responsiveness—and handling ease and comfort—he never imagined possible in a motor car. It is, in essence, an education in all the good things of motordom. If you are still looking forward to this extraordinary experience, we urge you to come in and see us at your earliest opportunity. The car is waiting for you—waiting to give you the most revealing ride of your life!

Your Cadillac Dealer

Our Love Affair with Cars

In the eight years since war's end, the US car industry had shifted from fabricating utilitarian war tanks and trucks, to producing fashionable consumer vehicles, the kind of which we just had to have.

There were now 46.3 million registered cars on US roads, up from 25.7 million at the end of WWII.[1] Our love affair with cars was firmly entrenched.

Mid-Afternoon Traffic on Broad Street, Philadelphia, early '50s.

Detroit had long been the car manufacturing hub of the country, and America led the world in car production, turning out 7.9 million vehicles in 1953 alone.[2]

Detroit's population had peaked in 1950, making it the fifth largest city in the US.[3] And by the end of the decade, a whopping one in six adults nation-wide would be employed in the car industry.

[1] fhwa.dot.gov/ohim/summary95/mv200.pdf.
[2] en.wikipedia.org/wiki/American_automobile_industry_in_the_1950s.
[3] theweek.com/articles/461968/rise-fall-detroit-timeline.

1953 Dodge Coronet V-Eight Convertible

Our love affair with cars grew hand-in-hand with the post-war baby boom and housing construction boom. Where would we be without our cars? How else could we commute from our outer-suburban homes to our inner-city offices?

Rising incomes ensured the family car was increasingly affordable. An additional 2.6 million vehicles were put on US roads during 1953 as families fled the cities for the quiet life of the suburbs.

1953 Packard Clipper

New! Big-Car Value At Medium-Car Cost!

Cars were no longer just a necessity; they had become an expression of our personality. Sturdy, sporty, or luxurious, cars now came in a wide range of styles, colors, and price points, with chrome, wings, stripes and fins for added personality.

Excitingly different! Studebaker's European look!

1953 Studebaker Commander V-8 hard-top, white sidewalls and chrome wheel discs.

Advertisement

The Distinguished DeSoto for 1953 with Power Steering, Power Braking, No-Shift Driving and World's Most Powerful Engine Design!

This distinguished DeSoto is a dramatic new concept in engineering and design! It's a longer car. It's lower. It's lovelier in every line. And its extraordinary performance is more than a match for its beauty.

Here is Full Power Steering that works *all* the time, that gives new control on the highway and makes parking as easy as dialing a telephone.

Here is DeSoto Power Braking for safer stops, with *half* the foot pressure.

Here is No-Shift Driving at its best. Famous chair-high seating. The luxury of huge, sweeping arcs of curved glass that mean a safer, better view.

And here is the revolutionary 160 h.p. Fire Dome V-8 (*the world's most powerful engine design!*) and the brilliantly responsive and economical Powermaster Six.

This new DeSoto is *your* car—if you're ready to take a great step forward in motoring. Just put it through its paces. You won't settle for anything less!

DeSoto Division, Chrysler Corporation   Famous for Fine Engineering

Advertisement

Another Engineering Miracle by Emerson!
Now! A TV picture so clear, so sharp...you'll think you're at the movies!

Emerson Space-Saver 21-inch models! The talk of the television world! The largest picture in the most compact cabinet ever built—and only Emerson gives it to you.

Unusual Fringe-Area Reception! The Emerson Dynapower Chassis gets even "difficult" stations sharp and brilliant as a "movie" picture! It *blocks out* "ghosts," shadows... *all* of the usual television nuisances!

New Exclusive Miracle Picture Lock... Actually *locks-in* your picture, then holds it steady, *all the time!* And you get this perfect reception with just one twist of your wrist, thanks to Emerson's *one-knob* Simplimatic tuning!

Ready Now for UHF! Built-in Antenna! Yes, Emerson gives you *more* in performance, *more* in value...and gives you 44 distinctive models to choose from, priced as low as $149.95.

The Secret! Emerson's exclusive, revolutionary *side controls* make the Space-Saver Cabinet possible. The front is all screen. A *full* 21" picture in the slimmest, trimmest cabinet ever built—*all* wood in blonde, mahogany, other fine finishes.

Emerson   America's Best Buy! Over 14,000,000 satisfied owners.

The Golden Age of Television

During the '50s, the television quickly became the centerpiece of every family home. By 1953, nearly 50% of the homes in the USA owned a TV set, (up from just 9% three years earlier).[1] And in the UK, TV sets were found in 25% of homes–many bought just in time to watch the Queen's Coronation. TV ownership continued to rise exponentially as television became our preferred choice of entertainment.

For the rising middle classes, television was much more convenient than going to a downtown cinema. It provided an increasing array of programs to watch, was available every day of the week, and it was free to watch once purchased. The rise of television spelled doom for the motion-picture industry. Cinema going audiences deserted downtown movie theaters in droves, forcing many to close.

[1] americancentury.omeka.wlu.edu/items/show/136.

Most Popular Television Shows of 1953

1	I Love Lucy	=	This Is Your Life
2	Dragnet	12	The Red Buttons Show
3	Arthur Godfrey's Talent Scouts	13	The Life of Riley
=	You Bet Your Life	14	Our Miss Brooks
5	The Milton Berle Show	15	Treasury Men in Action
6	Arthur Godfrey and His Friends	16	The Jack Benny Show
7	Ford Theatre	17	The Toast of the Town
8	The Jackie Gleason Show	18	Gillette Cavalcade of Sports
9	Fireside Theatre	19	Philco TV Playhouse
10	The Colgate Comedy Hour	20	The George Burns and Gracie Allen Show

* Nielsen Media Research 1953-'54 season of top-rated primetime television series in the USA.

During the first half of the 1950s, live television broadcasts from New York City dominated, based on radio and the theatrical traditions of Broadway. These were faster and cheaper to produce than new made-for-TV programs. However, situation-comedies, soap operas, and dramas, mostly created in Los Angeles, would soon become our primetime staples.

Lucille Ball with real life husband Desi Arnaz in *I Love Lucy* (CBS. 1950-1955).

Jack Webb (Sergeant Joe Friday) and Harry Morgan in *Dragnet* (NBC. 1951-1959).

Variety shows and situation-comedies remained the most popular forms of family-time TV entertainment, accounting for 12 of the top 20 programs for the year.

Also keeping us glued to our screens were highly rated drama series such as *Dragnet* (NBC. 1951-'59), *Ford Theatre* (NBC, ABC. 1948-'57), *Philco TV Playhouse* (NBC. 1948-'55) and *Fireside* (NBC. 1949-'58).

Ronald Reagan as host and part owner of *General Electric Theater* (CBS. 1953-1962).

Danny Thomas with Sherry Jackson in *The Danny Thomas Show* (ABC. 1953-'57, CBS. 1957-'64).

The television networks were quick to turn out new programs to keep us tuning in. Here are just a few of the new programs that aired for the first time in 1953: *General Electric Theater, Romper Room, The Danny Thomas Show* (originally *Make Room for Daddy*), *The Good Old Days* (BBC. 1953-'83), and *Panorama* (BBC. 1953-present).

Richard Dimbleby hosted *Panorama* from 1955 to 1965. It is the world's longest running news TV program (BBC. 1953-present).

Romper Room franchised its format nationally and internationally for filming with local children and a local host (1953-'94).

Enjoy "Eating Out" at Home! Serve Six for less than $1.00
Chun King Chow Mein and Chop Suey
Three Choices in Big New 3Lb. "Family-Economy" Size... Now at Your Grocers!

Here is Chow Mein at its rich, savory best. And so quick to fix. Just heat and serve over crisp Chun King Noodles or Rice. Six good big servings from the new "family-economy" size. Your choice of Chicken Chow Mein, Beef Chop Suey, Meatless Chow Mein. For a wonderful family dinner or when guests drop in–serve Chun King. Tonight? *Any night!*

Also available in 1 lb. cans to serve 2 or 3 persons... look for the Chun King foods section at your grocers.

Advertisement

"So lifelike you feel you're right there with 3 dimension pictures!"

The sensational Revere 3 Dimension Camera enables you to take amazingly lifelike pictures as easy as pie! Just press the button as you do with any ordinary camera. What you see, you catch in thrilling 3 dimensions. Everything has shape, form, depth! Full color scenes seem to spring to life with breath-taking 3 dimensional realism. So truly lifelike, viewers exclaim it's like being right there!

See the two lenses? They act like your eyes. Press button and they take two views of each scene. When viewed, scenes blend into 3 dimensions. Inexpensive—get 29 stereos from regular 35mm roll; 20 from special stereo film.

Even beginners get fine results from their first roll, so simple is Revere to operate! Guesswork is eliminated. Even focusing is automatic. Too, stereos are now mounted by your film processor and are returned to you ready to show!

Every picture's a thrill when viewed through the new Revere Viewer! It brings out the best in every shot! Ask your dealer to show you the new Revere Stereo Camera and Viewer.

For a new adventure in photography...Revere 33 Stereo Camera

Camera—2 matched, coated 35mm f/3.5 Revere Wollensak Amaton lenses with Revere Wollensak Kapax shutters; speeds ½ to ¹⁄₂₀₀; coupled focusing; internal synchro flash; superimposed image range-finder and viewer in camera head; double exposure preventive; single frame provision; level gauge. Inc. fed. tax $174.50. Viewer—fine achromatic lenses; both focusing and interocular adjustments; built-in light; 3-color plastic case. $18.50.

Eisenhower Inaugurated

20th January 1953

Dwight D. Eisenhower was inaugurated on 20th Jan to become the 34th president of the United States. He served two terms from 1953-1961 with Richard Nixon as his Vice President.

Eisenhower had been a life-long military man, rising to the rank of Army Chief of Staff. As he believed professional soldiers should abstain from seeking high political office, he maintained no political party affiliation. Prior to entering the presidential race, both the Democratic and Republican Parties pressed him to run for president. He chose to run for the Republican party, with Nixon as his running mate to appease the right-wing and appeal to the youth.

Eisenhower's White House portrait, 1959.

Eisenhower negotiated a truce in the Korean War only six months after taking office. As president he continued to work tirelessly to ease Cold War tensions. Domestically Eisenhower championed the construction of the Interstate Highway System. He enforced desegregation laws on transport and in schools, and secured racial integration in the Armed Services. He increased spending for space exploration, creating the space agency NASA.

Eisenhower considered himself a moderate, progressive Republican. His reputation and popularity has increased over time, as historians reveal more of his behind-the-scenes achievements.

Eisenhower taking the Presidential Oath of Office, administered by the Chief Justice of the USA the Honorable Frederick Vinson.

Death of a Dictator

5th March 1953

On 1st March, Joseph Stalin was found semi-conscious on the floor of his residence. He had suffered a cerebral hemorrhage. Four days later he was pronounced dead.

Stalin had been leader of the Soviet Union since 1922, and self appointed dictator since gaining absolute control of the Communist Party and government in the mid '30s. He ruled by terror, ensuring total domination by imprisoning or executing those who opposed him. An estimated 20 million people died as a result of his brutal rule.

Under Stalin's leadership, the USSR transformed from a peasant society to a military and industrial superpower. He ploughed funding into the development of nuclear weapons and space technology, cornerstones of the Cold War's Nuclear Arms Race and Space Race.

After his death, Stalin's body was embalmed and put on public display. Hundreds of thousands came to view the body, with such huge crowds that an estimated 100 people died by crushing.

China's Mao Zedong joins Stalin for his 71st birthday celebrations in Moscow, Dec 1949.

Advertisement

Now a round trip to Europe for $38 down! payment

Lowest TOURIST fares of year on "The Rainbow" — PLUS new "Pay-Later" Plan make your dream trip to Europe possible NOW

More people fly to Europe by PAN AMERICAN *World's Most Experienced Airline*

Living expenses in Europe are lower now... and you can include them, too, with the convenient new Pan Am "Pay-Later" Plan!

Your money talks *and in any language* offers these 4 reasons for going now—
- New "Pay-Later" Plan, originated by Pan Am, lets your pay just 10% down, the rest in 12 easy and convenient installments. The *nation-wide* credit plan for *world-wide* travel!
- Rainbow Clipper Tourist service actually saves you up to $200 over regular first-class service.
- And now, during "Thrift Season," the *Rainbow* saves you up to $300 (enough for 2 or 3 weeks in Paris!)
- "Thrift Season" living costs *in* Europe are amazingly low, too—you can live and sight-see in Paris for as little as $14 a day!

Listen to your money, it talks sense! It's not only easier and cheaper to go to Europe now, *it's more fun*, too. Theater, musicals, opera, social life—all are in full swing. Summer crowds are gone, the people are relaxed. It's Europe's gayest season.

Your entire trip can be financed under the Pan Am "Pay-Later" Plan: 10% down, the rest in modest monthly payments. *The "Pay-Later" Plan has now been extended so that it applies from 'most any city in the U.S.A. to anywhere in the world.*

East German Uprising

16th–17th June 1953

It began with a construction workers' strike against state determined production quotas on 16th June in East Berlin. Within 24 hours, over one million protestors in almost 700 localities joined in the action.

East German demonstrators demand free elections.

Soviet tanks roll into East Berlin, 17th Jun 1953.

With West Germany formalizing ties to Europe and America a year earlier, communist East Germany accelerated the "Sovietization" process of its political system and way of life.

Collectivization of farming land and factories had forced wealthy farmers, industrialists and professionals to flee to the West. The unproductive lands and factories resulted in food shortages, electricity outages, and general industrial unrest. The response by the governing Politburo was to increase the much hated production quotas, and increase prices for daily living costs, including food, healthcare and public transport.

As living standards declined, and with the economy in collapse, the Soviets demanded the Politburo immediately reverse the Sovietization policies, but the much hated production quotas were not renounced.

The protesters expanded their demands to include the resignation of the East German government, and free and fair Western-style elections. By the morning of 17th June, protests and riots had flared across the state. The Soviets were ready–declaring martial law, they brutally quashed the riots using massive military force.

Armistice Ends War in Korea

27th July 1953

American forces entered the Korean War in 1950, joined by a UN combined force from twenty-one countries including the UK, Australia, Canada, France, Philippines, and Thailand. Their purpose was to assist South Korea with expelling the communist invaders from the north. In contrast to the well equipped and well trained North Korean military (KPA), the South Korean forces were ill prepared and outnumbered.

With military backing from China and financial aid from the Soviets, the KPA crossed the boundary between the two Koreas at the 38th parallel in June 1950. They captured Seoul five times during the first 10 months of war. Each offensive was followed by a retreat, being pushed back by the UN allies towards the border with China.

Below: UN forces crossing the 38th parallel.
Bottom: A 1st Marine Division tank crew member climbs out to inspect his tank, 5th July 1953.

While the UN allies fought for a return to the Post War status quo of two Koreas divided along the 38th Parallel, the KPA was determined to unite Korea as one country under communist rule.

A two year stalemate, from July '51 to July '53, saw multiple battles of attrition waged, resulting in little or no progress on the ground.

In the air however, UN forces exploited their superior military power, dominating the skies. The US supplied much needed rocket launchers, anti-aircraft guns, jets, and bombers. US pilots conducted night-time bomb raids, venturing deep into North Korea to destroy enemy targets.

A total of 635,000 tons of bombs were dropped on North Korea, turning nearly every city and village to rubble. Citizens were advised to dig tunnels to live in. In addition, the US dropped 32,557 tons of lethal napalm.

Following the death of Stalin, political squabbling within Soviet ranks left little appetite for funding a war in Asia. Newly elected US President Eisenhower pushed forward with armistice talks.

The war unofficially ended on 27th July 1953 with the creation of the Demilitarized Zone separating the two Koreas. No peace treaty was ever signed, leaving the two Koreas technically still at war.

Casualties of war saw an estimated 1.68 million South Korean lives lost. Food shortages and lack of housing were severe. Casualties for the North Koreans and Chinese were even higher. Causes of death included bombings, massacres, starvation and disease.

Top to bottom: Soldiers boarding a U.S. Army Sikorsky H-19 Chickasaw helicopter.

Four US Marines stationed in Korea receive news of the Armistice.

Korean girl carrying her baby brother walks by a stalled M-46 tank at Haengju, 9th June 1950.

Advertisement

POTENT NORTH AMERICAN AJ "SAVAGE," POWERED BY TWO PRATT & WHITNEY PISTON ENGINES AND ONE JET, HAS MORE REACH THAN ANY OTHER CARRIER-BASED PLANE.

NAVY'S NEW SUB HUNTER-KILLER, THE GRUMMAN S2F, WILL DO JOB FORMERLY REQUIRING TWO AIRPLANES.

CHANCE VOUGHT'S NEW A2U, AN ATTACK VERSION OF CUTLASS TWIN-JET FIGHTER, WILL PACK MIGHTY PUNCH.

SWIFT DOUGLAS A3D IS THE LARGEST HEAVY ATTACK AIRPLANE NOW PLANNED FOR FUTURE CARRIER USE.

Since the outbreak of war in Korea, America has been working against time to build up its Air Power. Only our military leaders and Congress can decide how much Air Power we should have at any given time. Yet, as a leading manufacturer, we feel a responsibility to help you understand the vast complexity of modern aircraft... and why a "happy medium" level of production must be maintained in peace so that we can expand quickly to meet emergencies. Second-best Air Power is not enough in war. America's future security demands a long-range Air Power program in peace as well as in emergencies.

Potent North American AJ "Savage," powered by two Pratt & Whitney piston engines and one jet, has more reach than any other carrier-based plane.

Navy's new sub hunter-killer, the Grumman S2F, will do job formerly requiring two airplanes.

Chance Vought's new A2U, an attack version of Cutlass twin-jet fighter, will pack mighty punch.

Swift Douglas A3D is the largest heavy attack airplane now planned for future carrier use.

Advertisement

Zsa Zsa Gabor says, "C'est Magnifique...
No more ink-stained hands or clothes with my Paper-Mate Pen!"

Guaranteed Not to Leak! The Paper-Mate point is always clean and never needs wiping–retracts when not in use. Proved by daily use in more than 7000 banks. Proved by billions of words written by millions of users.

Guaranteed Not to Transfer! No more smeared writing. No more messy ink rubbing off onto fingers and back of hand. Paper-Mate's Ink is permanent on paper, yet if children write on clothes, the ink washes out easily.

Pick the Pen of Proved Performance! No other pen gives you such matchless writing luxury. No other pen has ever won such nationwide acclaim of bankers, teachers, aviators and mothers. So–insist on a genuine Paper-Mate Pen... copied by many, equalled by none.

Paper-Mate   Give Your Mate a Paper-Mate

Threat of Nuclear War

Cold War tensions between the two former allies—the USSR and the USA—dominated our lives throughout the '50s and '60s. Starting in the USA as policies for communist containment, the distrust and misunderstanding between the two sides quickly escalated from political squabbling, to a military nuclear arms race. For more than 40 years, the Nuclear Arms Race gave the two superpowers the pretext needed to test nuclear bombs on a massive scale.

At the end of 1952, the USA flexed its nuclear muscle by detonating the world's first superbomb—a thermo-nuclear fusion hydrogen bomb—one hundred times more powerful than those dropped on Hiroshima and Nagasaki. Code-named *Ivy Mike*, at 82 tons, it was too heavy to be deployed by air.

The Soviets responded in August 1953 with a layered thermonuclear bomb (part fusion, part fission). Known as RDS-6s (or Joe 4) this hydrogen bomb was light enough to be deployed from an aircraft.

With both sides H-bomb capable, Americans feared a nuclear war could start at any time. Citizens built bomb shelters, and nuclear bomb drills became commonplace.

Both superpowers increased their stockpiles of nuclear weapons. US stockpiles peaked in 1966 with a total of 31,175 against the Soviet's 7,089 weapons.[1] The USSR continued to grow their stockpile until 1988. In 1991, the Nuclear Arms Race ended with the signing of a denuclearization treaty.

Las Vegas tourist postcard from the early-'50s promoting views of nuclear testing at the Nevada Proving Grounds.

[1] tandfonline.com/doi/pdf/10.2968/066004008.

Execution of the Rosenbergs

19th June 1953

Convicted of espionage, Julius and Ethel Rosenberg were executed at the Sing Sing Correctional Facility in Ossining, New York, on 19th June. They were charged with spying on behalf of the Soviet Union, by providing top-secret information on jet propulsion engines, radar, sonar, and valuable nuclear weapon designs. They were condemned to die in the electric chair, making them the only two American civilians to be executed for espionage-related activity during the Cold War.

Julius Rosenberg was accused of leading a network of spies, several of whom had been arrested earlier on suspicion of passing top-secret information to the Soviets. Ethel Rosenberg was accused of assisting in her husband's spy network.

Julius and Ethel Rosenberg, separated by heavy wire screen in the US Court House, after being found guilty by jury, 1951.

Protests and campaigns to prevent the executions occurred throughout the year, by those who believed the Rosenbergs were innocent, or their sentence too harsh. Many public figures including Albert Einstein, Jean-Paul Sartre, Pablo Picasso, and Pope Pius XII unsuccessfully appealed to the president.

Documents released decades later proved Ethel Rosenberg's role in her husband's activities were minor and limited. Her conviction and execution were wrongful. She had been framed by her brother and sister-in-law, who were themselves spies in the same network.

Advertisement

Mothers and Daughters Doing Fine
Many work together in telephone offices in communities throughout the country

It happens over and over again. A daughter sees how much her mother likes her telephone job and decides she would like to work there, too. So in she comes to put in her application.

When daughter follows mother, and brother follows sister, and son follows father, you get a pretty good line on how people feel about the telephone company.

They know from firsthand experience that "it is a good place to work."

In Her Mother's Footsteps—"Mother did all right and I hope to do as well," says Telephone Operator Betty Miller. She's shown here with her mother, Mrs. Ruby Miller, a telephone Service Assistant.

Like Mother. Like Daughter. Betty Johnson (left) is a Service Order Typist in the same telephone building where her mother, Mrs. Dena Johnson, is Business Office Supervisor. Mrs. Johnson's aunt and cousin are telephone employees, too.

A Telephone Family. Mrs. Grace M. Donewald, an Instructor, visits her mother, Mrs. Grace Franks, a Special Commercial Clerk. Her father, a telephone Commercial Engineer, has recently been assigned as a Defense Activities Co-ordinator.

Bell Telephone System... *"A Good Place to Work"*

Advertisement

Now Millions Know! One King Size tops 'em all for Taste and Comfort!
Your throat can tell–it's Philip Morris

No matter what brand you're now smoking... there's greater pleasure waiting for you in the new Philip Morris King-Size. Millions of smokers who tried them are buying them over and over again! Once you try them, you will, too. Because *your throat can tell* that here, at last, is a cigarette not only good to *smoke*... but good to the *smoker*... good to *you!* Try a carton–*now!*

Lucille Ball starring in the Lucille Ball, Desi Arnaz "I Love Lucy" Show CBS-TV

1953 in Cinema and Film

Deborah Kerr and Burt Lancaster in *From Here to Eternity* (Columbia Pictures, 1953).

Highest Paid Stars
1. Gary Cooper
2. Dean Martin & Jerry Lewis
3. John Wayne
4. Alan Ladd
5. Bing Crosby
6. Marilyn Monroe
7. James Stewart
8. Bob Hope

Having reached its peak in the mid-1940s, cinema attendance faced a steady decline throughout the 1950s. With more and more families filling their leisure time with the convenience of television, the motion-picture industry sought new ways to win over new audiences.

Younger audiences now had cash to spare. Movie themes adjusted to accommodate the trends in popular culture, and to exploit the sex appeal of young, rising stars such as Marilyn Monroe, James Dean and Marlon Brando.

Steve McQueen in *The Great St. Louis Bank Robbery* (United Artists, 1959).

Dean Martin, Jerry Lewis and Marilyn Monroe at the 1953 Redbook Awards.

1953 film debuts

Carroll Baker	Easy to Love
Harry Belafonte	Bright Road
Steve McQueen	Girl on the Run
Anthony Perkins	The Actress
Maureen Stapleton	Main Street to Broadway
Stanley Kubrick (director)	Fear and Desire

* From en.wikipedia.org/wiki/1953_in_film.

Top Grossing Films of the Year

1	The Robe	20th Century Fox	$17,500,000
2	From Here to Eternity	Columbia Pictures	$12,200,000
3	Shane	Paramount Pictures	$8,000,000
4	How to Marry a Millionaire	20th Century Fox	$7,300,000
5	Peter Pan	Walt Disney/RKO	$6,000,000
6	House of Wax	Warner Bros. Pictures	$5,500,000
7	Gentlemen Prefer Blondes	20th Century Fox	$5,100,000
8	Salome	Columbia Pictures	$4,750,000
9	Mogambo	MGM	$4,576,000
10	Knights of the Round Table	MGM	$4,518,000

* From en.wikipedia.org/wiki/1953_in_film by box office gross in the USA.

Fictional biblical epic *The Robe* was the first movie to be filmed using widescreen CinemaScope. Starring Richard Burton and Jean Simmons, the film was a critical and box office success.

Marilyn Monroe starred in two 1953 blockbusters: *How to Marry a Millionaire* and *Gentlemen Prefer Blondes*.

Advertisement

Marilyn Monroe says, "Yes, I use Lustre-Creme Shampoo" When America's most glamorous women use Lustre-Creme Shampoo, shouldn't it be your choice above all others, too?

Now! Lustre-Creme Shampoo also in New Lotion Form!

Never before—a liquid shampoo like this! Lustre-Creme Shampoo in new Lotion Form is much more than just another shampoo that pours. It's a new creamy lotion, a fragrant, satiny, easier-to-use lotion, that brings Lustre-Creme glamour to your hair with every heavenly shampoo!

Voted "Best" in dramatic use-tests!—Lustre-Creme Shampoo in new Lotion Form was tested against 4 leading liquid and lotion shampoos...all unlabeled. And 3 out of every 5 women preferred Lustre-Creme in new Lotion Form over each competing shampoo tested00for these important reasons:

• Lather foams mor quickly! • Easier to rinse away! • Cleans hair and scalp better! • Leaves hair more shining! • Does not dry or dull the hair! • Leaves hair easier to manage! • Hair has better fragrance! • More economical to use!

Pour it on—or cream it on! In famous Cream Form, Lustre-Crème is America's favorite cream shampoo. And all its beauty-bringing qualities are in the new Lotion Form. Whichever form you prefer, lanolin-blessed Lustre-Crème will leave your hair shining clean, eager to wave, never dull or dry.

1953 Sci-Fi Inspired Films   Advertisement

War of the Worlds by Paramount.   *Project Moonbase* by Galaxy Pictures Inc.

It Came from Outer Space by Universal Pictures.   *Planet Outlaws* by Universal Pictures.

Advertisement

Every model a 3-in-1 camera... a black-and-white camera... a color camera... and a flash camera
 Today's Kodak cameras are "luxury" cameras at down-to-earth prices... built with the knowledge gained through 65 years of giving people more and more picture-making pleasure for the least money.
 Finer lenses and shutters give crisper, clearer snap-shots. Simple, easy-working controls mean years and years of trouble-free snapshot fun. Dollar for dollar... feature for feature... you're buying the best... when you buy a camera marked "Kodak" or "Brownie."
 Brownie Hawkeye Camera $7.20. Gets crisp, clear snapshots the surest, simplest way. No adjustments... just line up your picture to the oversize finder and press the button. Makes 12 snaps per roll. Flasholder extra, $4.
 Kodak Duaflex II Camera $14.50. Shows you your picture big and clear–*before* you snap. Flip-up hood brightens image in viewfinder. As simple to operate as a Brownie camera. Gets 12 crisp snapshots per roll. Flasholder extra, $4.25.
 Kodak Pony 135 Camera $35.75. A 35mm miniature that gets color slides as crisp and brilliant as cameras costing twice as much. You can project them big and bright–and have beautiful color prints made from them. Fast, color-corrected $f/4.5$ lens, 1/200-second shutter. Settings specially marked in red make it as simple to operate as a box camera. Loads with 20- or 36-exposure films. Kodak Pony 828 Camera, 8-exposure model, $31.15. Flasholder, $8.25.
 Kodak Tourist II Camera $26.25. Smart new model of an old favorite, the folding camera. Easy to take along on trips and outings. Built-in flash makes indoor pictures easy to get. Has modern eye-level finder for split-second sighting, squeeze-action shutter release for steady shooting. Prefocused lens. Takes eight horizontal or vertical pictures per roll. Flasholder extra, $8.25.

James Bond 007 in Print

13th April 1953

The post-war spy thriller *Casino Royale* was the first book by British author Ian Fleming. The book centered around the exploits of British spy James Bond (007), an officer of the British Secret Intelligence Service (MI6). Fleming would release one James Bond novel per year until his death in 1964, with an additional two novels released posthumously. Several short stories were also written, many of which fill the plot gaps between novels.

Prior to writing, Fleming worked in Britain's Naval Intelligence Division during the second world war. His years in service gave him ample inspiration for plots and characters to use in his books.

Ian Fleming reading Casino Royale.

Casino Royale introduced us to a number of characters who appear regularly in subsequent books, including M as head of MI6, Miss Moneypenny as M's assistant, MI6's Chief of Staff Bill Tanner, and French agent René Mathis.

Notable to all 007 books is the Bond Girl (love interest or partner of 007), and the dastardly villain, of which there are always one or more.

Poster for the first James Bond movie *Dr. No* starring Sean Connery and Ursula Andress, (United Artists, 1962). Connery starred as 007 in seven Bond movies from 1962-1983.

All twelve of Fleming's Bond novels, and a number of his short stories, have been made into feature films. Since Fleming's death, books written by other authors commissioned to carry on the Bond series have also been adapted for film. Securing the role of Bond, or a Bond Girl, is a considered badge of honor for any actor or actress.

Musical Memories

Music of the early '50s was smooth and mellow, with lyrics focused on story telling and expressing heartfelt emotion. Frank Sinatra, Dean Martin, Bing Crosby, Perry Como, Nat King Cole, Tony Bennett, Sammy Davis Jr. and Charles Azanavour headed the line-up of early '50s classic pop crooners. Their velvety voices led us to joyous highs and the depths of despair. We had yet to fully embrace the electrifying beats of rock 'n' roll.

Music of the early '50s fell into one of three distinct styles—country, R&B, and pop music. In 1953, there was little crossover between the styles. Radio stations focused on one genre, allowing listeners easy access to their preferred type of music.

Bing Crosby's career spanned more than five decades. As a singer, actor, television producer, television and radio personality and businessman, he was a global cultural icon.

Eddie Fisher and actress Debbie Reynolds at their wedding, 1955.

Teen idol Eddy Fisher released ten singles in 1953, in addition to hosting his own variety TV series *Coke Time with Eddie Fisher* (NBC. 1953–1957). In future years, his good looks and popularity would be overshadowed by his controversial private life. He is now best remembered for his high-profile marriages to actresses Debbie Reynolds and Elizabeth Taylor.

Advertisement

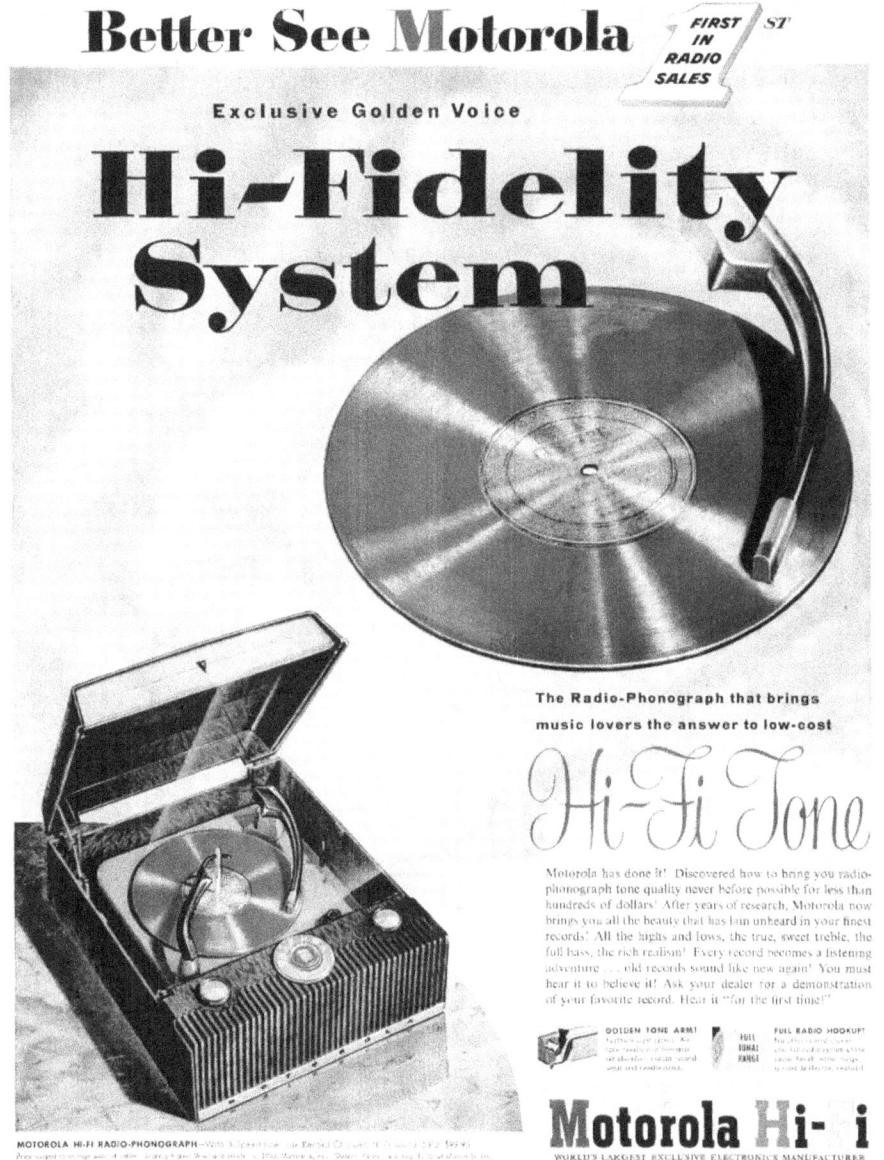

Better See Motorola Exclusive Golden Voice Hi-Fidelity System

The Radio-Phonograph that brings music lovers the answer to low-cost Hi-Fi Tone

Motorola has done it! Discovered how to bring you radio-phonograph tone quality never before possible for less than hundreds of dollars! After years of research, Motorola now brings you all the beauty that has lain unheard in your finest records! All the highs and lows, the true, sweet treble, the full bass, the rich realism! Every record becomes a listening adventure... old records sound like new again! You must hear it to believe it! Ask your dealer for a demonstration of your favorite record. Hear it "for the first time!"

Motorola Hi Fi   World's Largest Exclusive Electronics Manufacturer

1953 Billboard Top 30 Songs

	Artist	Song Title
1	Percy Faith	The Song from Moulin Rouge
2	Les Paul & Mary Ford	Vaya con Dios
3	Patti Page	(How Much Is) That Doggie in the Window?
4	Eddie Fisher	I'm Walking Behind You
5	Ames Brothers	You, You, You
6	Teresa Brewer	Till I Waltz Again with You
7	Les Baxter	April in Portugal
8	Perry Como	No Other Love
9	Perry Como	Don't Let the Stars Get in Your Eyes
10	Frankie Laine	I Believe

Perry Como, 1956.

Eddie Fisher, 1960.

Frankie Laine, 1954.

Patti Page.

	Artist	Song Title
11	Pee Wee Hunt	Oh
12	Frank Chacksfield	Ebb Tide
13	Nat King Cole	Pretend
14	Richard Hayman	Ruby
15	Stan Freberg	St. George and the Dragonet
16	The Hilltoppers	P.S. I Love You
17	The Gaylords	Tell Me You're Mine
18	Julius La Rosa	Eh, Cumpari!
19	Tony Bennett	Rags to Riches
20	Silvana Mangano	Anna

Tony Bennett.

Nat King Cole, 1958.

21	Perry Como	Say You're Mine Again
22	Ray Anthony	Dragnet
23	Jimmy Boyd & Frankie Laine	Tell Me a Story
24	June Valli	Crying in the Chapel
25	Joni James	Why Don't You Believe Me?
26	Joni James	Your Cheatin' Heart
27	Frank Chacksfield	Limelight (Terry's Theme)
28	Eddie Fisher	With These Hands
29	Eartha Kitt	C'est si bon
30	Joni James	Have You Heard?

* From the *Billboard* top 30 singles of 1953.

Advertisement

"Let your own mirror show you..." says Mrs. William H. Miles, another lovely Woodbury bride.

Use the Soap Made with Face Cream Oils... New Woodbury Soap!

Now you can have the cleanest, most radiant complexion of your life!

Woodbury skin scientists have found a way to blend 7 face cream oils *right into* each cake of New Woodbury Soap! (The same oils and emollients used in costly face creams!) They're intended to help *replace* natural oils you wash away–oils so necessary for smooth and young-looking skin.

And New Woodbury Soap is a delight in other ways, too. It gives more generous billows of rich, creamy lather. More gentle, more thorough cleansing! The cake itself is a beautiful, clear, sea-spray green color. And the delicate new bridal-flower fragrance clings delightfully. Altogether, New Woodbury Soap is the loveliest beauty care you ever used!

Get New Woodbury Soap in its new blue and white wrapper with the lovely lady and her mirror. It's the symbol of an exquisite, new complexion for you! (And, P.S.— on the big bath size New Woodbury, it's the symbol of new all-over loveliness.)

Now better than ever! 'Woodbury Soap for the skin you love to touch!'

Advertisement

Florida Fashions

Direct-by-mail to You for Greater Savings. Satisfaction Guaranteed or your money back

New! Exciting! Fashions
for now... for Easter and right thru Summer

Richer, Crisper, Rustling Taffeta.
Looks expensive! Feels expensive! Sizes 10 to 22 $6.98

Fashion Trends of the 1950s

With the misery and bleakness of the war years behind us, it was now time to show off. Consumerism was a way of life and we were all too willing to spend money on luxuries, non-essentials, and fashion.

How we looked and how we dressed became important everyday considerations for women and men. We spent money like never before, guided by our favorite fashion icons, and helped along by a maturing advertising industry which flooded us with fashion advice through newspapers, magazines, billboards, radio and television.

Distinction magazine cover, Summer 1953.

Clothing manufacturers had perfected mass production techniques while providing military uniforms during the war years. They now shifted their focus to well made, stylish, ready-to-wear clothes.

Seventeen magazine cover, June 1953.

Ebony magazine cover, June 1953.

Vogue magazine cover, 1st May 1953.

Fashion was no longer a luxury reserved for the wealthy. Now the growing middle class could also afford to be fashionable. Magazines and mail-order catalogs kept us informed of the latest trends in fashion, make-up, and accessories.

Advertisement

Dresses from the *Bellas Hess* mail order catalog in the "New Look" style that was popular in the year 1953.

Advertisement

You'll look so naughty—feel so nice in Warner's Merry Widow

Warner-Wonderful for New Year's Eve—or any eve when you want to look *little* wanton! It's the one, the only—the *original* Cinch-bra that took the country by storm.

Takes as much as two inches from your waist! Shapes the most bewitching curves with comfy wires *under* the bust so the sheer bra cuffs can dip *surely*, sensationally low.

See for yourself. *Everything nice* happens to the girl who starts her holidays in Warner's Merry Widow! In misty black or white nylon marquisette and elastics. #1311 at $12.50.

And the more the *merrier!* Look for a whole family of Warner's styles, inspired by this fabulous flatterer—strapless bras to lacy corselettes. Now at your nicest stores, here and in Canada.

Warner's   Bras • Girdles • Corselettes

Christian Dior's "New Look" from 1947.

The New Look in *Vanity Fair*, May 1953.

As with before the war, all eyes looked to Paris for new trends in haute couture. In 1947 Christian Dior didn't disappoint, unveiling his ultra-feminine, glamorous, extravagant, "New Look".

Gone were the boxy tailored jackets with padded shoulders and slim, short skirts. Paris had brought back femininity, with clinched waists, fuller busts and hips, and longer, wider skirts.

By 1953, dresses reached voluminous proportions with pleats and folds flaunting an abundance of fabric. The New Look set the standard for the entire decade of the 1950s.

how clever!

EVEN THE WIRE IS CURVED TO STAY UP!

CELEBRITY does more than give you deep-plunging separation... CELEBRITY curves the wiring of this strapless bra to make the uplift STAY UP! No tugging, no pulling, no displacement! Get marvelous up-curve flattery in heavenly comfort. White rayon satin, or white cotton.

A Cup, sizes 32 to 36
B Cup, sizes 32 to 38

$1.50

Celebrity "CONTOUR-CURVE STITCHING" from the bottom up

To achieve this impossible hourglass figure, corsets and girdles were sold in record numbers. Metal underwire bras made a comeback, and a new form of bra known as the "cathedral bra" or "bullet bra" became popular.

Despite criticisms against the extravagance of the New Look, and arguments that heavy corsets and paddings undermined the freedoms women had won during the war years, the New Look was embraced on both sides of the Atlantic. Before long, inexpensive, ready-to-wear versions of Dior's New Look had found their way into our department store catalogs.

Patterns from *Haslam Dresscutting Book*, Autumn & Winter 1953.

Advertisement

now playing everywhere
dangerous... dynamic... Jantzen "curvallure"

Nothing like Jantzen "curvallure" has happened to you before. It's the magic you've been wanting to make you look wonderful, feel wonderful in a swim suit... an exclusive new Jantzen technique for creating lovely curves and planes in all the right places. This suit is Latex-powered faille loaded with "curvallure" from the top of its heart-shaped neckline to the cuffs of its pant-legs 16.95.

Famous Jantzen racer, Lastex faille 4.95

Jantzen best of all swim suits

nothing does as much for a girl as a Jantzen

Dior also created a slimmed down alternative look, as a sleek dress or elegant straight skirt with short jacket. This figure-hugging, groomed and tailored look, known as the sheath dress, continued to place emphasis on the hourglass figure.

Also known as the "wiggle dress", this sexier figure-hugging silhouette was preferred by movie stars such as Marilyn Monroe.

Women embraced the femininity of 1950s fashion from head to toe. Hats, scarves, belts, gloves, shoes, stockings, handbags and jewelry were all given due consideration.

Out on the street, no outfit would be complete without a full complement of matching accessories.

Not much changed in the world of men's fashion during the 1950s. Business attire shifted just a little. Suits were slimmer, and ties were narrower. Skinny belts were worn over pleated pants. Hats, though still worn, were on the way out.

Marlon Brando.

Frank Sinatra.

James Dean.

For the younger generation however, the fashion icons of the day set the trends. James Dean and Marlon Brando made the white T-shirt and blue jeans the must-have items in casual attire. Worn alone, or under an unbuttoned shirt or jacket, the look made working class style a middle-class fashion statement.

Advertisement

The neatest Christmas gift of all!, says Ronald Reagan
You can twist it... You can twirl it... You can bend it... You can curl it...
The new revolutionary collar on Van Heusen Century shirts won't wrinkle ever!
Ronald Reagan starring in Universal International's "Law and Order," Color by Technicolor

The Van Heusen Century is the *only shirt in the world* with a soft collar that *won't wrinkle... ever!* It fits smoothly always, without starch or stays.

Soft as a fine handkerchief, and as easy as launder—because the fold-line is *woven in*. Just iron the collar flat, flip it, and it folds perfectly every time.

Also, it gives you up to *twice the wear* of ordinary shirts. Whites, $3.95. Superfine Whites and colors, $4.95. Tie shown: Van Heusen Shirt-Mate, $1.50.

A Vaccine for Polio

26th March 1953

On 26th March, American medical researcher Dr. Jonas Salk confirmed he had developed a vaccine against polio. His research involved testing the vaccine on former polio patients, and on himself and his family, before announcing his success on national radio. Dr. Salk became an immediate celebrity.

During the first half of the 20th Century, the dreaded poliomyelitis virus (polio) caused frequent epidemics throughout the industrialized world. The virus appeared during the summer months, attacking mostly the young, causing muscle weakness, paralysis and death.

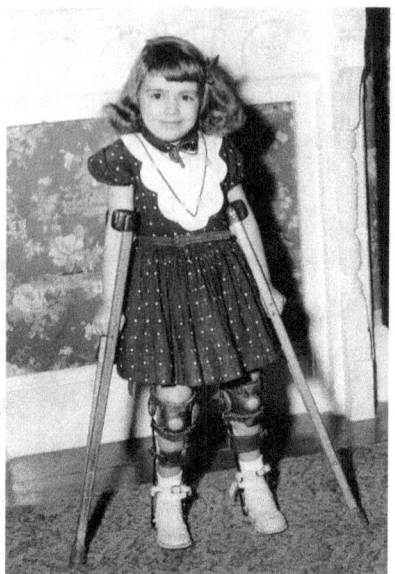

A young polio patient—Elaine Burns, age 5, with her braces in 1957.

At its peak in the '40s and '50s, polio affected many thousands of people each year. Use of the "iron lung" a pressure chamber to aid breathing, saved the lives of those with infected lungs. Patients were encased within for months, years, or even for life.

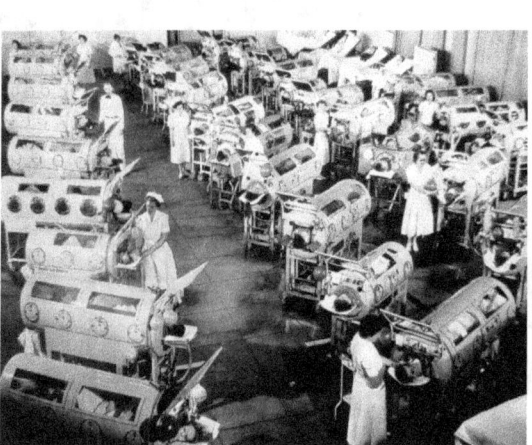

Rows of polio patients in their iron lungs, Rancho Los Amigos hospital in Downey, Calif. 1953.

To save on floor space within polio wards, children were placed in iron lung "pods"— multi-person negative-pressure ventilators.

Worldwide polio eradication is still an ongoing struggle, as some developing countries continue to see yearly outbreaks of the virus. Civil wars, ignorance, and government distrust prevent large scale vaccination programs from succeeding.

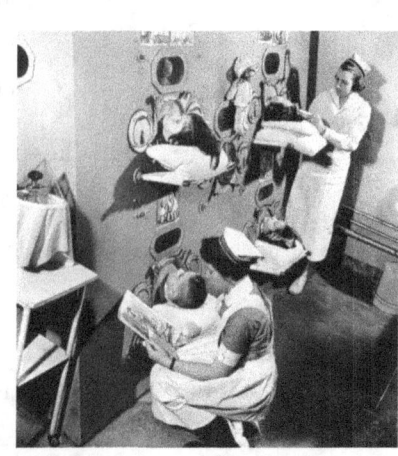

Technology and Medicine

28th Feb– James Watson and Francis Crick announced their discovery of the double helix structure of the DNA molecule. In April they published their results in the British journal *Nature*, along with DNA X-ray results by Maurice Wilkins. The trio would receive a shared Nobel Prize for Medicine ten years later.

17th Mar– 1,620 spectators watch the first nuclear test of Operation Upshot–Knothole in Nevada, from an assumed safe distance of 3.4 km (2.1 mi).

11th Apr– The US Department of Health, Education and Welfare was established with Oveta Culp Hobby as Secretary. She would be the second woman in history to achieve this rank.

6th May– Cardiac surgeon John H. Gibbon performed the world's first successful open heart surgery using a heart-lung machine, which could take over the functions of these vital organs.

4th Sep– The discovery of REM sleep is first published by researchers Eugene Aserinsky and Nathaniel Kleitman.

29th Oct– Inge Edler and Gustav Hertz, recorded the first moving pictures of the heart using a borrowed ultrasonic reflectoscope. This paved the way for the field of ultrasound cardiography.

Advertisement

Crosley "Skymaster" has its own genuine cowhide carry case. Cleverest carry case ever designed! Lets you reach the dials—tune the radio as it lightly swings from your shoulder. Made of genuine top-grade leather with a costly "hand-stitched" look, in fashion-right rich russet shade. Available at slight extra cost.

The sensational new Crosley Skymaster costs only $39.95 less batteries.

Be the first in your group to own this exciting portable *clock* radio!

Have music wherever you go—lolling in a hammock, out camping, or down by the seashore! Leave your expensive watch at home; this Crosley portable has its own accurate clock. Set it—and your favorite program comes on automatically. Take a sunbath; a special bell alarm calls you any moment you say.

The Crosley "Skymaster" is a beauty! And though it's scarcely bigger than a book, the speaker is *two and a half times larger* than most personal portables. You know that means far better tone. An Indoor-Outdoor Switch gives you greater clarity outdoors. And you get more playing time. Thanks to a special Power-Saver Switch, one set of batteries will last *through an entire season* with average use!

Five dazzling colors: Red, Black, Chartreuse, Blue, Green.

Look at all the other wonderful, colorful Crosley Radios

Advertisement

Spring never leaves Acapulco and you'll never want to!

No matter how long you plan to stay, Acapulco promises you an unforgettable vacation. A warm sun that never deserts it and a 12-month season of serene days and gay, romantic nights have made this Mexican seaside resort the "Riviera" of the Western Hemisphere. You'll fish, sail, swim and sun on Acapulco's lovely beaches. And dance the night away in Acapulco's famed hotels. No wonder you never want to leave Acapulco! But when you do, remember, you're only a few hours from home thanks to daily Flagship service all year long.

American Airlines   America's Leading Airline

Sporting Events from 1953

11th Jan– J. Edgar Hoover declined a 6-figure offer to become chairman of the International Boxing Club board of directors.

4th Mar– British soccer player Tommy Taylor was transferred from Barnsley to Manchester United, for a record sum of £29,999.

12th Apr– Ben Hogan shattered the Masters scoring record by 5 strokes with 274 (–14) at the 17th US Masters Tournament. He would win three majors in 1953, the equivalent of a modern-day Grand Slam.

15th May– Rocky Marciano KOs Jersey Joe Walcott in the 1st round to defend his world heavyweight title.

13th Jun– British runner Jim Peters became the first athlete to run a marathon in under 2 hours 20 mins (2:18:40.2).

12th Aug– Ann Davison became the first woman to sail solo across the Atlantic.

19th Aug– The England cricket team defeated Australia to take back The Ashes for the first time in 19 years.

23rd Aug– Italian Alberto Ascari won the F1 driver's championships for the second time driving a Ferrari.

7th Sept– Maureen Connolly Brinker became the first woman to win a Women's Grand Slam. In the history of tennis only Margaret Court (1970) and Steffi Graff (1988) have achieved this title to date.

Everest Conquered

29th May 1953

On 29th May, New Zealand Mountaineer Edmund Hillary and Sherpa Tenzing Norgay from Nepal reached the summit of Mount Everest. This was the ninth attempt to conquer the world's highest mountain. It was a feat that for centuries had been deemed impossible.

Hillary and Norgay after successfully completing the first ascent of Mount Everest, 29th May '53.

The climbers were part of a British expedition led by Colonel John Hunt. The team of 350 (mainly porters), required 16 days to walk from Kathmandu, with another 21 days at a high altitude to acclimatize.

Hunt planned for three attempts to reach the summit, with climbers in pairs. Teams of Sherpas moved tons of supplies up to Base Camp, and from there to a few higher altitude camps. The first pair set out on 26th May, successfully reaching the South Summit at 1 pm. Exhausted, with oxygen supply problems and lack of time, they turned back at 1.20pm. They had set a new record, just 100 m (300 ft) shy of the summit.

Hillary and Norgay set out early on 29th May, passing the South Summit at 9am, and reaching the Summit at 11.30am. Spending some time to take photos, the pair left a crucifix and some food offerings before returning to camp.

A coded message was used to wire news of the climb back to London. The joyful news of their success reached London on the morning of the Queen's Coronation. Hillary and Hunt were awarded knighthoods from the Queen, with a Georges Medal given to Norgay.

Other News from 1953

31st Jan-1st Feb– The North Sea flood killed 1,836 people in southwestern Netherlands, 307 in the UK and 133 at sea on the ferry MV Princess Victoria. Maynard Sinclair, Northern Ireland's Minister of Finance, was among the dead.

13th Mar– The Academy Awards was televised for the first time, live from New York and Hollywood simult-aneously. An estimated 34 million televiewers tuned in to watch the event.

14th Jan– Josip Broz Tito became president of Yugoslavia.

18th Jun– A US Air Force plane crashed just after take-off near Tokyo, Japan, killing all 129 on board, making it the worst air crash to date.

5th Aug– Following the end of the Korean War, American prisoners were repatriated under the prisoner swap known as Operation Big Switch.

12th Aug– A 7.2 magnitude earthquake devastated several Greek islands.

19th Aug– The Iranian military staged a coup d'état, overthrowing the democratically elected Prime Minister of Iran. The coup had support of the USA and UK.

20th Aug– The United States returned 382 ships to West Germany which had been captured during World War II.

12th Sep– Jacqueline Bouvier married John F Kennedy at St. Mary's Church in Newport, Rhode Island. An estimated 700 guests attended the ceremony, with 1,200 at the reception. The event was the social event of the season.

Dec– Lesney Products of London began selling Matchbox toy vehicles.

The 1953 Queen Elizabeth II Coronation Coach was one of the first Matchbox cars to be created and was hugely successful, selling over one million copies.

24th Dec– A railway bridge collapsed at Tangiwai, New Zealand. 151 passengers were killed when a fully loaded passenger train plunged into the river below.

Dec– Hugh Hefner's Playboy Magazine began publication, featuring nudes of Marilyn Monroe in its first issue. 54,175 copies sold for $.50 each.

If you like beer You'll Love Schlitz
No harsh bitterness... Just the kiss of the hops

This dry and mellow beer... this beer of *matchless flavor*... is the world's largest seller.

Year after year more bottles and cans of Schlitz are bought—*millions more*—than of any other beer. This popularity is the result of the most conclusive taste test in beer history.

Schlitz is available in quartz bottles, 12-oz. bottles and cans, and the 7-oz. bottle. Also in 24-Pak and handy 6-Pak cartons of cans and "one-way" bottles that require no deposit.

On TV every week—The popular "Schlitz Playhouse of Stars."

Advertisement

Special! (From Borden's!) For Penny-Wise Housewives (and Good Cooks, too!)

For only 9¢ a quart Borden's Starlac makes good, healthful nonfat milk. *S-t-r-e-t-c-h* your food budget with top-quality milk... minus the fat. That's what Starlac does. Just add Starlac to water—beat or shake. Keep at least a quart of Starlac in the refrigerator at all times. Tastes mighty good with any meal. Us it in all your "made-with-milk" recipes. Get Starlac at your grocer's today!

Secret of better coffee—Rich tasting Borden's is 100% Pure Crystals of 100% Pure Coffee. Why does Borden's Instant Coffee make such good coffee... so rich-tasting... so different from ordinary ground or instant kinds? Because it is 100% pure coffee, crystalized... with only the water removed. Put back the water... crystals dissolve instantly. You've *fresh* coffee—and you save up to 25¢ over a lb. of ground coffee. Buy Borden's Instant Coffee at your grocer's.

All a-board! All a-Borden's. Elsie saves you "Moo-la" on the Good Food Line! Borden foods must be good—more folks buy food packages carrying the Borden's brand name than any other in the world.

Famous People Born in 1953

10th Jan– Pat Benatar [Andrezejewski], American singer.

19th Jan– Desi Arnaz Jr., American actor & musician.

21st Jan– Paul Allen, American business magnate (co-founder Microsoft) (d. 2018).

22nd Jan– Jim Jarmusch, American director.

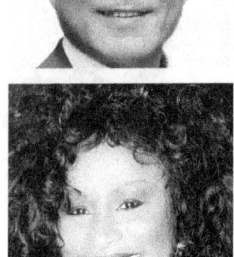

24th Jan– Moon Jae-in, South Korean politician & President (2017-22).

26th Feb– Michael Bolton [Bolotin], American singer & songwriter.

23rd Mar– Chaka Khan [Yvette Marie Stevens], American singer & songwriter.

16th Apr– Peter Garrett, Australian environmentalist, activist, politician and musician (Midnight Oil)

18th Apr– Rick Moranis, Canadian actor.

23rd Apr– James Russo, American actor.

6th May– Tony Blair, British politician & Prime Minister (Labour: 1997-2007).

8th May– Alex Van Halen, Dutch-American rock drummer.

16th May– Pierce Brosnan, Irish actor.

24th May– Alfred Molina, British Actor.

5th Jun– Kathleen Kennedy, American film producer & President of Lucasfilm (2012-).

15th Jun– Xi Jinping, President of China (2013-).

21st Jun– Benazir Bhutto, Pakistani politician & President (d. 2007).

22nd Jun– Cyndi Lauper, American singer.

10th Jul– Françoise Bettencourt Meyers, French author & L'Oréal heiress.

19th Jul– Howard Schultz, American businessman, CEO of Starbucks.

23rd Jul– Graham Gooch, English cricketer & captain.

29th Jul– Tim Gunn, American television & fashion personality.

8th Aug– Nigel Mansell, British auto racer.

11th Aug– Hulk Hogan [Terry Bollea], WWF heavyweight champion (1984-89).

16th Aug– Kathie Lee Gifford, American TV presenter, singer, songwriter, actress & author.

16th Aug– James "J.T." Warren Taylor, American R&B singer (Kool & the Gang).

11th Sep– Renée Geyer, Australian singer.

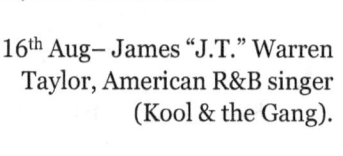

22nd Sep– Ségolène Royal, French politician.

15th Oct– Tito Jackson, American singer (Jackson 5).

8th Dec– Kim Basinger, American actress.

9th Dec– John Malkovich, American actor.

13th Dec– Ben Bernanke, American economist & Chairman of the Federal Reserve (2006-14).

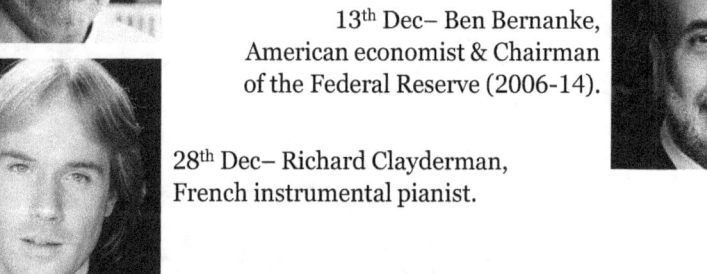

28th Dec– Richard Clayderman, French instrumental pianist.

Advertisement

You like it... it likes you!

THE ALL-FAMILY DRINK!

Get a family supply of 24 bottles. Buy 7-Up by the case. Or get the handy 7-Up Family Pack. Easy-lift center handle, easy to store. Buy 7-Up where you see the bright 7-Up signs.

"Fresh up" with Seven-Up!

Really got a grip on that 7-Up, haven't you, big boy? Go right ahead, "fresh up" to your heart's content! Mom knows sparkling, crystal-clear 7-Up is so pure, so good, so wholesome that folks of *all ages*—even little guys like you—can enjoy it often!

You like it... it likes you!   The All-Family Drink!

Get a family supply of 24 bottles. Buy 7-Up by the case. Or get the handy 7-Up Family Pack. Easy-lift center handle, easy to store. Buy 7-Up where you see the bright 7-Up signs.

Really got a grip on that 7-Up, haven't you, big boy? Go right ahead, "fresh up" to your heart's content! Mom knows sparkling, crystal-clear 7-Up is so pure, so good, so wholesome that folks of *all ages*–even little guys like you–can enjoy it often!

"Fresh up" with Seven-Up!

1953 in Numbers

Census Statistics [1]:

- Population of the world   2.68 billion
- Population in the United States   165.91 million
- Population in the United Kingdom   50.75 million
- Population in Canada   14.83 million
- Population in Australia   8.78 million
- Average age for marriage of women   20.2 years old
- Average age for marriage of men   22.8 years old
- Average family income USA $4,200 per year
- Unemployment rate USA   4.5 %

Costs of Goods [2]:

- Average new house	$18,159
- Average new car	$1,650
- Packard, Clipper	$2,679
- A gallon of gasoline	$0.27
- Margarine	$0.29 per 4 oz
- A loaf of bread	$0.16
- Peanut butter	$0.29
- Beef, porterhouse steak	$0.89 per pound
- Lamb, leg	$0.59 per pound
- Oranges, Florida	$0.55 per 5 pounds
- Potatoes	$0.29 per 10 pounds
- SPAM	$0.45 per 12 oz can
- Soap, Ivory	$0.19 per 4 cakes
- Drive-in movie	$1.00 per car

1 Figures taken from worldometers.info/world-population, US National Center for Health Statistics, Divorce and Divorce Rates US (cdc.gov/nchs/data/series/sr_21/sr21_029.pdf) and United States Census Bureau, Historical Marital Status Tables (census.gov/data/tables/time-series/demo/families/marital.html).
2 Figures from thepeoplehistory.com, mclib.info/reference/local-history & dqydj.com/historical-home-prices/.

Advertisement

Each season is right for this lighter-weight

Let autumn zero into winter and winter mellow into spring—you'll weather all seasons smartly in this all-year lighter-weight Champ Dash. There's a blend of airiness, style and four-season comfort throughout its superbly crafter 3 ounces. Smoothly fashioned from imported Kashmir fur-felt. And pre-creased to keep a fresh-from-the-hatbox shape in smog, rain or sleet. Is it time you had a new hat, a comfortable hat?

Champ Dash is yours, individually boxed, for only $7.50. Other Champ lighter-weights and regular-weights, $7.50, $8.50, $10 and $12.50. At men's stores and department stores everywhere.

Advertisement

For a great vacation Pacific Northwest by way of Glacier National Park
Vacation all the way...Go Streamlined Empire Builder or Western Star

New vistas await you in the majestic Pacific Northwest!...the Cascades and the Colombia... Puget Sound and Mt. Rainier. On your way, stop in Glacier Park, in the Montana Rockies. See it all on one great trip. Go carefree, be carefree. Go Great Northern!

Write P. G. Holmes, Great Northern Ry., Dept. N-43, St. Paul 1, Minn., for details on a Western "Vacation-of-a-Lifetime."

• Glacier Park served only by Western Star, June 15 thru September 10.

These words first appeared in print in the year 1953.

- DRIP-DRY
- UFO
- Heart-lung machine
- digitize
- SUNBLOCK
- flea collar
- encryption
- Global warming
- Videotape recorder
- Road trip
- ballpoint pen
- overqualified
- half-marathon
- fracking
- skateboard
- SLUMLORD
- Male-pattern baldness

*From merriam-webster.com/time-traveler/1953.

A heartfelt plea from the author:

I sincerely hope you enjoyed reading this book and that it brought back many fond memories from the past.

Success as an author has become increasingly difficult with the proliferation of **AI generated** copycat books by unscrupulous sellers. They are clever enough to escape copyright action and use dark web tactics to secure paid-for **fake reviews**, something I would never do.

Hence I would like to ask you—I plead with you—the reader, to leave a star rating or review on Amazon. This helps make my book discoverable for new readers, and helps me to compete fairly against the devious copycats.

If this book was a gift to you, you can leave stars or a review on your own Amazon account, or you can ask the gift-giver or a family member to do this on your behalf.

I have enjoyed researching and writing this book for you and would greatly appreciate your feedback.

Best regards,
Bernard Bradforsand-Tyler.

Please leave a
book review/rating at:

https://bit.ly/1953-reviews
Or scan the QR code:

Flashback books make the perfect gift- see the full range at

https://bit.ly/FlashbackSeries

Image Attributions

Photographs and images used in this book are reproduced courtesy of the following:

Page 6 – From *Life* Magazine 16th Mar 1953.
Source: books.google.com/books?id=F0IEAAAAMBAJ&printsec (PD image).*
Page 8 – From *Life* Magazine 2nd Nov 1953.
Source: books.google.com/books?id=IEgEAAAAMBAJ&printsec (PD image).*
Page 9 – From *Life* Magazine 2nd Nov 1953.
Source: books.google.com/books?id=IEgEAAAAMBAJ&printsec (PD image).*
Page 10 – From *Life* Magazine 8th Jun 1953.
Source: books.google.com/books?id=3EcEAAAAMBAJ&printsec (PD image).*
Page 11 – From *Life* Magazine 5th Jan 1953. Source: books.google.com/books?id=QUIEAAAAMBAJ&printsec (PD image).* – Magazine cover by Science Service Inc.
Source: comicbookplus.com/?cbplus= atomic. Pre 1978, no mark (PD image).
Page 12 – From *Life* Magazine 2nd Mar 1953.
Source: books.google.com/books?id=E0IEAAAAMBAJ&printsec (PD image).*
Page 13 – The Gold State Coach on Coronation Day. Source: commons.wikimedia.org/wiki/Category: Coronation_of_Elizabeth_II. License CC BY-SA 2.0 (PD image).
Page 14 – London aerial by Sunshine34, commons.wikimedia.org/wiki/File:London_1953.jpg. License CC BY-SA 3.0 (PD image). – Classroom photo, Creator unknown. Pre 1978, no mark (PD image).
Page 15 – Churchill portrait, source: en.wikipedia.org/wiki/Winston_Churchill#/media/File:Sir_Winston_Churchill_-_19086236948.jpg by Yousuf Karsh for Library and Archives Canada, e010751643 (PD image). – Churchill with Queen Elizabeth II, Prince Charles and Princess Anne, 10th Feb 1953. Source: commons. wikimedia.org/wiki/File:Churchill_queen_ Elizabeth_1953.jpg. Pre 1978 (PD image).
Page 16 – From *Life* Magazine 15th Jun 1953.
Source: books.google.com/books?id=A0gEAAAAMBAJ&printsec (PD image).*
Page 17 – Coronation portraits of Queen Elizabeth II,
source: commons.wikimedia.org/wiki/Category:Coronation_of_ Elizabeth_II (PD images).
Page 18 – From *Life* Magazine 3rd Aug 1953.
Source: books.google.com/books?id=W0IEAAAAMBAJ&printsec (PD image).*
Page 19 – Traffic, creator unknown. Source: theoldmotor.com/?p=171594. Pre 1978 (PD image).
Page 20 – Dodge Coronet V-8 Convertible from *Life* Magazine 13th Jul 1953.
Source: books.google.com/books?id=ZEIEAAAAMBAJ&printsec (PD image).* – 1953 Packard Clipper from *Life* Magazine 9th Feb 1953. Source: books.google.com/books?id=FkIEAAAAMBAJ&printsec (PD image).* – Studebaker Commander (1953) from *Life* Magazine 12th Oct 1953.
Source: books.google.com.sg/books?id=pEYEAAAAMBAJ&printsec (PD image).*
Page 21 – From *Life* Magazine 2nd Feb 1953.
Source: books.google.com/books?id=KUIEAAAAMBAJ&printsec (PD image).*
Page 22 – From Life Magazine 2nd Nov 1953.
Source: books.google.com/books?id=IEgEAAAAMBAJ&printsec (PD image).*
Page 23 – Artists impression of family TV time for Bendix Solo-Ear Imperial TV in mahogany console. From Life Mag 7th Dec '53. Source: books.google.com/books?id=O0kEAAAAMBAJ&printsec (PD image).*
Page 24 – Screen still from I Love Lucy, by CBS Broadcasting,** taken from the book I Love Lucy: Celebrating 50 years of Love and Laughter, by Elisabeth Edwards, Running Press Book Publishers, 2010. Source: Library of Congress (097.01.00). [Digital ID # lucy0097_02]. – Screen still from Dragnet, NBC Television** 30th August 1957, source: en.wikipedia.org/wiki/ Dragnet_(1951_TV_series).
Page 25 – General Electric Theatre, 1955 by CBS.** Source: en.wikipedia.org/wiki/General_Electric_Theater. – The Danny Thomas Show, source: en.wikipedia.org/wiki/The_Danny_Thomas_Show. (PD image).** – Panorama, screen still, Richard Dimbleby by BBC.** – Romper Room publicity, 1953 by Claster Television.**
Page 26 – From Life Magazine 16th Feb 1953.
Source: books.google.com/books?id=JUIEAAAAMBAJ&printsec (PD image).*
Page 27 – Revere 33 Stereo Camera print advertisement. Source: eBay (PD image).*
Page 28 – Eisenhower official portrait from the Eisenhower Presidential Library, 29th May 1959.
Source: commons.wikimedia.org/wiki/Dwight_D._Eisenhower (PD image).* – Inauguration, 20th Jan 1953. Source: inaugural.senate.gov/42nd-inaugural-ceremonies/ (PD image).*
Page 29 – Joseph Stalin at Potsdam Conference, 1st Aug 1945. Photo by US Army Signal Corps, from the US Library of Congress' Prints and Photographs-digital ID cph.3a14367 (PD image). – Stalin with Mao, Nikolai Bulganin, Walter Ulbricht and Mongolia's Yumjaagiin Tsedenbal.
Source: commons.wikimedia.org/wiki/File:1949_Mao_and_Stalin.jpg (PD image).
Page 30 – Pan Am print advertisement, 1953. Source: eBay (PD image).*
Page 31 – Protestors and Soviet tanks in the streets of Berlin, 16th-17th Jun 1953. Creator unknown.
Source: militaryhistories.co.uk/berlin/revolt. Both images pre 1978, no copyright mark (PD image).

Page 32 & 33 – UN forces withdraw from Pyongyang, crossing the 38th parallel, by U.S. Information Agency, creator unknown. From the National Archives and Records Administration, cataloged under the National Archives Identifier (NAID) 541822. – A 1st Marine Division tank crew member is careful not to let the hatch door slam against his tank, as he climbs out to inspect his tank after received three harmless 76 Howitzer hits. NARA FILE #: 127-GK-234D-A173204 ID: 127GK234DA173204. By MSGT. J.W. Hayes– Helicopter in Korea, 1953, by PFC E. E. Green, U.S. Army - NARA FILE#: 111-SC-422077. – US soldiers read of the Armistice to be signed the next day. AP photo used under fair use terms. This photo is relevant to the article created and is too small for reproduction by others. – Korean girl carrying her brother, by Maj. R.V. Spencer, UAF (Navy), 8th June 1951. From the National Archives and Records Administration, National Archives Identifier (NAID) 520796. All photos source: commons.wikimedia.org/wiki/Korean_War. All photos these pages are the work of US Army Soldiers, US Marines or their employees and are in the public domain.

Page 34 – From *Life* Magazine 4th May 1953.
Source: books.google.com/books?id=L0kEAAAAMBAJ&printsec (PD image).*
Page 35 – From Life Magazine 4th May 1953.
Source: books.google.com/books?id=L0kEAAAAMBAJ&printsec (PD image).*
Page 36 – Ivy Mike by The Official CTBTO, source: flickr.com/photos/ctbto/6476282811/. – Las Vegas tourism postcard from the early '50s, creator unknown. Photos this page pre 1978, no mark (PD image).
Page 37 – Rosenbergs by Roger Higgins, source: www.loc.gov/resource/cph.3c17772/ (PD image).
Page 38 – From Life Magazine 6th Apr 1953.
Source: books.google.com/books?id=4EgEAAAAMBAJ&printsec (PD image).*
Page 39 – From Life Magazine 6th Jul 1953.
Source: books.google.com/books?id=DEgEAAAAMBAJ&printsec (PD image).*
Page 40 – Screen still from From Here to Eternity, by Colombia Pictures 1953.**– Still image from video of The Redbook Awards, 1953.** – McQueen, still image from The Great St. Louis Bank Robbery (1959).** Source: en.wikipedia.org/wiki/Steve_McQueen.
Page 41 – The Robe, 1953 film poster by 20th Century Fox.** – Gentlemen Prefer Blondes, 1953 film poster by 20th Century Fox.** – How to Marry a Millionaire, 1953 film poster by 20th Century Fox.**
Page 42 – Lustre-Creme Shampoo print advertisement. Source: eBay (PD image).*
Page 43 – War of the Worlds, 1953 movie poster by Paramount.** – Project Moonbase, 1953 movie poster by Galaxy Pictures Inc.** – It Came from Outer Space, 1953 movie poster by Universal Pictures.** – Planet Outlaws, 1953 movie poster by Universal Pictures.**
Page 44 – From *Life* Magazine 1st Jun 1953.
Source: books.google.com/books?id=30cEAAAAMBAJ&printsec (PD image).*
Page 45 – Publicity photo of Ian Fleming reading *Casino Royale*, for Jonathan Cape publishing. Source: ianfleming.com. – *Dr. No* movie poster by EON Productions, 1962. **
Page 46 – Bing Crosby studio portrait, 1951 for CBS (PD image). – Wedding of Fisher and Reynolds, 1955, creator unknown. Source: commons.wikimedia.org/wiki/Category:Eddie_Fisher (PD image).
Page 47 – From *Life* Magazine 12th Oct 1953.
Source: books.google.com/books?id=pEYEAAAAMBAJ&printsec (PD image).*
Page 48 – Perry Como by NBC Television, 1956. Source: commons.wikimedia.org/wiki/File:Perry_Como_1956.JPG. – Eddie Fisher studio publicity photo, source: commons.wikimedia.org/wiki/Category:Eddie_Fisher. – Frankie Laine publicity photo, 1954. Source: en.wikipedia.org/wiki/Frankie_Laine. – Patti Page source: wikivisually.com/wiki/Patti_Page by General Artists Corporation. All images this page permission PD-PRE1978.
Page 49 – Tony Bennet promotional photo for the song *Rags to Riches*, Colombia Records, 1953. – Nat King Cole publicity for GAC-General Artists Corporation.
Source: commons.wikimedia.org/wiki/File:Nat_King_Cole_ 1958.JPG. (PD image).
Page 50 – From *Life* Magazine 6th Apr 1953.
Source: books.google.com/books?id=4EgEAAAAMBAJ&printsec (PD image).*
Page 51 – *Florida Fashions* mail catalog, 1953. Source: likesoldclothes.tumblr.com/tagged/1953/ (PD image).*
Page 52 – From Distinction magazine cover, Summer 1953.
Source: likesoldclothes.tumblr.com/tagged/1953/ (PD image).*
Page 53 – Fashion magazine covers from 1953. Pre 1978, no copyright mark (PD image).*
Page 54 – *Bellas Hess* Catalog 1953, (PD image).*
Page 55 – From *Life* Magazine 7th Dec 1953.
Source: books.google.com/books?id=O0kEAAAAMBAJ&printsec (PD image).*
Page 56 – From *Vanity Fair,* May 1953. Source: likesoldclothes.tumblr.com/tagged/1953/ (PD image).*
Page 57 – Celebrity advert from *Life* Magazine 1st Jun 1953. Source: books.google.com/books?id=30cEAAAAMBAJ&printsec (PD image).* – *Haslam Dresscutting* patterns, Autumn & Winter No.30, 1953. Pre 1978 (PD image).*
Page 58 – From *Life* Magazine 8th Jun 1953.
Source: books.google.com/books?id=3EcEAAAAMBAJ&printsec (PD image).*
Page 59 – Marilyn Monroe in 1952 studio publicity portrait for film *Niagara*, by 20th Century Fox. (PD image). – Models walking photo. Source: Jessica at myvintagevogue.com. Licensed under CC BY 2.0.
Page 60 – Sinatra, source: morrisonhotelgallery.com/collections/wtvp8g/The-Sinatra-Experience-. – Brando, source: dailybreak.co/wp-content/uploads/2019/06/Marlon-Brando-Ford-Thunderbird-1955-Est.-2444.jpg. – Dean, source: en.wikipedia.org/wiki/James_Dean. All images this page Pre-1978, no mark (PD image).
Page 61 – From *Life* Magazine 14th Dec 1953.
Source: books.google.com/books?id=PkkEAAAAMBAJ&printsec (PD image).*

Page 62 – Young girl, source: polioplace.org/history/artifacts/reluctant-poster-child. Pre-1978, no mark (PD image). – Iron Lung ward, source: commons.wikimedia.org/wiki/File:Iron_Lung_ward-Rancho_Los_Amigos_ Hospital.gif by fda.gov (PD image). – Children's ward, source: imgur.com/gallery/vdwfM40. Pre-1978, no copyright mark (PD image).
Page 63 – Watson and Crick in 1959, creator unknown. – Nevada - Frenchman's Flat - members of 11th AB Div. kneel on ground to watch mushroom cloud of atomic bomb test in 1951. From the US Library of Congress. Source: loc.gov/resource/cph.3a47482/. – Edler and Hertz with the loaned ultrasound reflectoscope, creator unknown. All images this page Pre-1978, no copyright mark (PD image).
Page 64 – From *Life* Magazine 15th Jun 1953.
Source: books.google.com/books?id=A0gEAAAAMBAJ&printsec (PD image).*
Page 65 – From *National Geographic* Magazine, Vol. 103, No. 3, Mar 1953 (PD image).*
Page 66 –Rocky Marciano, source: commons.wikimedia.org/wiki/Category:Rocky_Marciano. – Jim Peters, screenshot from TV footage, creator unknown. Source: sporting-heroes.net/athletics. – Maureen Connolly, source: commons.wikimedia.org/wiki/Category:Maureen_Connolly. All photos this page are in the Public Domain.
Page 67 – Tenzing Norgay and Edmund Hillary, 29th May 1953.
Source: commons.wikimedia.org/wiki/File:Edmund_Hillary_and_Tenzing_Norgay.jpg. (PD image).
Page 68 – North Sea Flood, 1953. Creator unknown. – Academy Awards poster by RCA Victor, 1953.** – Royalists, carrying a picture of the shah, rode a commandeered bus in Tehran on 19th Aug 1953. Source: commons.wikimedia.org/wiki/Category:1953_Iranian_coup. Images are included here for information only under US fair use laws due to: 1- images are low resolution copies; 2- images do not devalue the ability of the copyright holders to profit from the original works in any way; 3- Images are too small to be used to make illegal copies for use in another book; 4- The images are relevant to the article created.
Page 69 – Jackie Bouvier and John F. Kennedy married in Newport, Rhode Island, on 12th Sep 1953. Source: commons.wikimedia.org/wiki/File:Kennedy_marriage.jpg (PD image). – 2nd version Large Coronation Coach by Lesney Toys, 1973 Matchbox series. Source: harveys-matchbox.de/Lesney05. – Cover of *Playboy* magazine 1st issue, Dec 1953.**
Page 70 – From *Life* Magazine 1st Jun 1953.
Source: books.google.com/books?id=30cEAAAAMBAJ&printsec (PD image).*
Page 71 – From *Life* Magazine 2nd Feb 1953.
Source: books.google.com/books?id=KUIEAAAAMBAJ&printsec (PD image).*

Page 72-74 – All photos are, where possible, CC BY 2.0 or PD images made available by the creator for free use including commercial use. Where commercial use photos are unavailable, photos are included here for information only under US fair use laws due to: 1- images are low resolution copies; 2- images do not devalue the ability of the copyright holders to profit from the original works in any way; 3- Images are too small to be used to make illegal copies for use in another book; 4- The images are relevant to the article created.
Page 75 – From *Life* Magazine 9th mar 1953. Source:
books.google.com/books?id=GUIEAAAAMBAJ&printsec (PD image).*
Page 78 – Champ Dash print advertisement. Source: eBay (PD image).*
Page 79 – Great Northern Railway print advertisement. Source: eBay (PD image).*

*Advertisement (or image from an advertisement) is in the public domain because it was published in a collective work (such as a periodical issue) in the US between 1925 and 1977 and without a copyright notice specific to the advertisement.
**Posters for movies or events are either in the public domain (published in the US between 1925 and 1977 and without a copyright notice specific to the artwork) or owned by the production company, creator, or distributor of the movie or event. Posters, where not in the public domain, and screen stills from movies or TV shows, are reproduced here under USA Fair Use laws due to: 1- images are low resolution copies; 2- images do not devalue the ability of the copyright holders to profit from the original works in any way; 3- Images are too small to be used to make illegal copies for use in another book; 4- The images are relevant to the article created.

This book was written by Bernard Bradforsand-Tyler as part of *A Time Traveler's Guide* series of books.

All rights reserved. The author exerts the moral right to be identified as the author of the work.

No parts of this book may be reproduced, stored in any retrieval system, or transmitted in any form or by any means, without prior written permission from the author.

This is a work of nonfiction. No names have been changed, no events have been fabricated. The content of this book is provided as a source of information for the reader, however it is not meant as a substitute for direct expert opinion. Although the author has made every effort to ensure that the information in this book is correct at time of printing, and while this publication is designed to provide accurate information in regard to the subject matters covered, the author assumes no responsibility for errors, inaccuracies, omissions, or any other inconsistencies herein and hereby disclaims any liability to any party for any loss, damage, or disruption caused by errors or omissions.

All images contained herein are reproduced with the following permissions:
- Images included in the public domain.
- Images obtained under creative commons license.
- Images included under fair use terms.
- Images reproduced with owner's permission.

All image attributions and source credits are provided at the back of the book. All images are the property of their respective owners and are protected under international copyright laws.

First printed in 2022 in the USA (ISBN 978-1-922676-06-1).
Revised in 2024, 2nd Edition (ISBN 978-1-922676-20-7).
Self-published by B. Bradforsand-Tyler.

www.ingramcontent.com/pod-product-compliance
Lightning Source LLC
Chambersburg PA
CBHW072104110526
44590CB00018B/3309